The History Detective
Investigates Local History

J907.2

Alison Cooper

W

HODDER
Wayland

An imprint of Hodder Children's Books

For more information on this series, go to www.hodderwayland.co.uk

This book was originally written by Martin Parsons and first published in 1997 by Wayland Publishers Ltd.

This edition was simplified and updated by Alison Cooper in 2004 by Hodder Wayland, an imprint of Hodder Children's Books

© Hodder Wayland 2004

British Library Cataloguing in Publication Data
Cooper, Alison
  The history detective: investigates local history
  1. Local history - Research - Juvenile literature
  2. History- Sources - Juvenile literature
  1. Title
  907.2
  ISBN 0 7502 46758

Printed and bound in China

Editor: Victoria Brooker
Designer: Simon Borrough
Cover design: Hodder Children's Books

The publishers would like to thank the following for permission to reproduce their pictures:
Cover pictures: Hodder Wayland Picture Library
David Beasley, Pie Powder Press 24 (bottom), 25 (bottom); Peter Cox, Fotosparks 7 (bottom-left), 17, 24 (top), 25 (top), 40 (bottom); James Davis Travel 36; Edinburgh Central Library 12, 13, 15; Eye Ubiquitous 41 (top); Robert Harding 4, 32; Huntly House Edinburgh 9; Oxford Picture Library 8; Edward Parker 5; Martin Parsons 26, 27; Popperfoto 22; Sheffield City Museums 19 (bottom); Tony Stone 33, 44; Topham 7 (bottom-right); 20, 21, 41 (bottom), 43, 45; Wayland Picture Library 1, 6, 7 (top), 19 (top), 23, 37, 38, 39, 40 (top), 42; Welsh Industrial and Maritime Museum 28, 29, 30, 31
Cartoon bloodhound by Richard Hook
Illustrations on pages 34, 35 and 37 by John Yates

The website addresses (URLs) included in this book were valid at the time of going to press. However, because of the nature of the Internet, it is possible that some addresses may have changed, or sites may have changed or closed down since publication. While the authors and Publishers regret any inconvenience this may cause the readers, no responsibility for any such changes can be accepted by either the author or the Publisher.

Contents

Words in **bold** can be found
in the glossary.

Introduction

Finding out about the past is a bit like being a detective. You have to search for clues, just like the famous storybook detective Sherlock Holmes. When you have found several clues, you can put them together to build up a picture of what happened in the past.

Often, the quickest way to find out about the past is to look in a history book or on a website. But you can't always do this if you are trying to find out about the area you live in, or investigating your own house, because the information isn't usually available there. You have to do the detective work yourself. This book will explain how to do it.

These large buildings in Kent are oast houses. People live in them today, but when they were first built they were places for drying hops.

HOP FIELDS

You can use Sherlock Bones, our cartoon dog detective (below right), to help with your project. He will show you how to:
- choose a history mystery to investigate
- find the missing clues
- take short cuts and save time.

By the end of the book you should be able to put together your evidence and write your report – just like a real detective.

 The buildings, the signpost and the pub sign below all give you clues about an industry that used to be very important in Kent. Can you find out what the industry was?

Wherever you see a paw print like this, you will find a mystery to solve – to help you practise your detective skills. The answers are on page 47.

ISLE OF DOGS

CHARRINGTON

IN GOD IS ALL OUR TRUST

BREWERS ARMS

Look closely at the shield on the pub sign to get more clues.

Choosing your topic

When you are choosing your topic to investigate, you might find it easiest to start with a question. This will help you to think about the sort of clues you need to look for.

For example, if you want to find out about your house, you might call your project 'Who has lived in my house?' Then you can investigate the people who lived in the house before you. Did they have large families? What kind of jobs did they do? Were they rich or poor? Did they live to be very old, or did they die when they were young?

By asking questions like these, you can find out whether their lives were similar to yours, or different. You will discover how to find the information as you read this book.

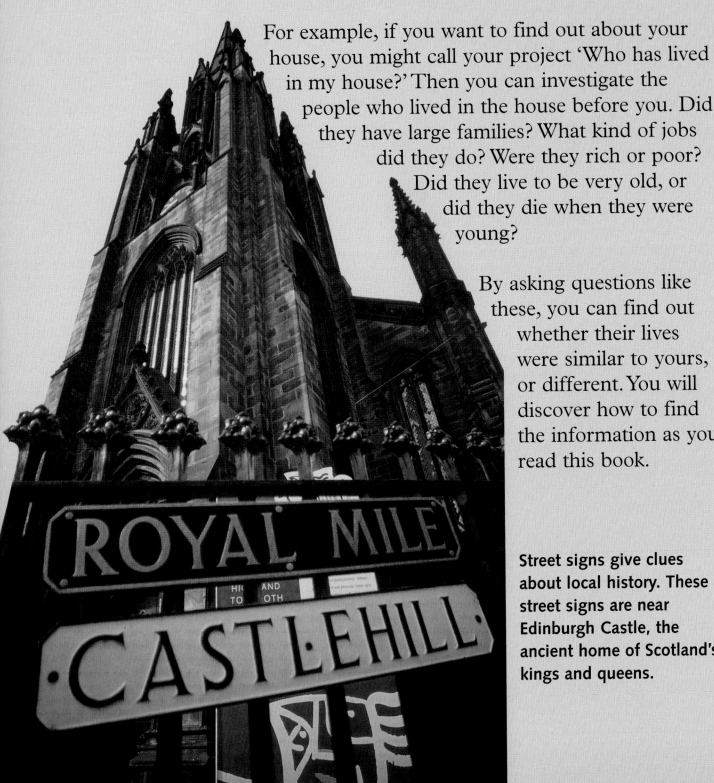

Street signs give clues about local history. These street signs are near Edinburgh Castle, the ancient home of Scotland's kings and queens.

The report in this old newspaper is a useful clue.

Other starting points for your investigation could be:
● Does my town's name give a clue to its history?
● Why does a road have a certain name?
● What is the story behind the person shown in a local statue?
● How did the local pub get its name?

Choose a project that you can investigate by looking at primary sources. Primary sources are things from the past like buildings, newspapers, photographs and written records. Most important of all – choose a project that you will enjoy.

How do you think these streets in Reading got their names?

The picture on the pub sign is an extra clue.

Clues all around you

Perhaps you can't think of a place that would make a good topic for your history investigation? If so, why not take a closer look at the buildings and monuments in your local area. You might find a fascinating topic – right under your nose!

This is an unusual well in Oxfordshire. Can you work out where it might have come from? Look at its shape and the writing on it.

HIS HIGHNESS THE MAHARAJAH OF BENARES

If possible, take a camera or a sketch pad with you and go on a history walk. Look out for unusual details on buildings. There might be a name or date over the door, unusual windows, or strange marks on the walls. Make a quick drawing or take a photograph. Remember – you are a history detective and you need to search carefully for clues.

🐾 These metal signs are from Huntly House in Edinburgh. They would have been very important if the house caught fire. Can you find out why houses had signs like these?

Searching the records

Sometimes you need to look for evidence in old books and **documents**. To do this, you have to look in the library or the local **Record Office**, and you will probably need to ask an adult to help you. Here's Sherlock Bones to explain how to find exactly what you need when you visit the Record Office.

1 Look up the county council in your phone book and find the number for the Record Office. When you ring up, ask the **archivist** who looks after the records if they have the document you need. If they do, you need to arrange a time to go and look at it.

2 Go to the Record Office at the time you have arranged. The archivist will give you a reader's ticket, which you need to sign. Keep it safe, because you can use it next time you come.

3 Most Record Offices keep their records on computer. If not, you will have to look in the index cards.

Imagine you want to find the school logbook for Crookham School in the **parish** of Thatcham in Berkshire for the year 1880.

Thatcham School Records

1864–1964	Logbooks of Thatcham Church of England School	C/EL 53/1, 2-6
1875–1957	Logbook of Crookham School	C/EL 36/1-3
1794-1860	Minutes and Accounts of Lady Winchcombe's Charity School	D/P 130/25/6
1913-1955	School Manager's Minutes	C/EM 19, 67
1900-1957	Crookham C of E (Controlled) School	C/EZ 7
1945-1946	Registers of British School, Senior, Junior and Infant Departments	C/ER 32

The Parish Index lists the parishes in a county in alphabetical order. If you know which parish the school is in, you can find it in this index.

The Subject Index contains a list of subjects in alphabetical order. To find a school logbook, you have to look under 'Education'.

C/EL/Education: School Logbooks 3- Berkshire Record Office

29	Burghfield Common (Mrs Bland's)	1 vol.	1873-1905
30/1,2	Didcot, The Manor School, C of E	2 vols.	1881-1903
31	Didcot, Board (Evening School)	1 vol.	1896-1904
32	Didcot, Board (Infant's Class)	1 vol.	1887-1918
33	Woolhampton, C of E		
34/1, 2	Maidenhead, Boyne Hill	2 vols.	1866-1905
35, 1/2	East Hagbourne, C of E	2 vols.	1875-1954
36/1-3	Crookham (parish of Thatcham)	3 vols.	1875-1957

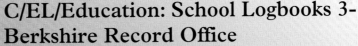

36/1

What is the reference number for the Crookham school logbook? It is shown in both indexes.

When you have found the reference number, you have to fill in a request form. Give it to the archivist and he or she will find the logbook and bring it to you. You can then look through it for the evidence you need for your project.

Street directories

If you live in a town, you might find important evidence for your project by looking in a street directory. You can find these in your local reference library.

Street directories contain advertisements for shops and other businesses, like this one.

Street directories list all the houses in a street. They also show the names of the **householders** and sometimes the types of job they did. This can give you some good clues about the important trades and industries in your area.

Look at the examples below and on the next page. They are from the street directories for Edinburgh and Leith in 1882–3 and 1883–4. The Grassmarket is an area in the centre of Edinburgh.

Grassmarket, Edinburgh, 1882–3

1	Richardson, Francis, & Co		60	M'Donald, Angus, saddler
5	Scott, James, & Co		58	Rose, William, saddler
7	Lindsay, John		56	Edinburgh Rope, Bag, and Twine Store
9	Spence, Joseph, saddler		54	Wilkinson, John
11 & 13	Spence, Henry B.		54	Thomson's Court
15	Traynor, John, rag merchant		54	M'Ewan, Robert
19	McCallum, Alexander Inglis		52	Forgan, David, grocer

Grassmarket, Edinburgh 1883-4

1	Richardson, Francis, & Co	60	M'Donald, Angus, saddler
5	Scott, James, & Co	56 & 58	Rose, William, saddler
7	Lindsay, John	54	Wilkinson, John
9	Spence, Joseph, saddler	54	Thomson's Court

The street directory for 1882–3 shows that there were three saddlers in the street: Joseph Spence, Angus M'Donald and William Rose.

The street directory for the next year, 1883–4, shows that William Rose has taken over Number 58 as well as Number 56. His business must have been successful.

A. & J. MAIN & CO.,
IRON FENCE, GATE, AND BRIDGE MANUFACTURERS,
WIRE-WORKERS, ETC.,
CORN EXCHANGE BUILDINGS, 31 GRASSMARKET

A. & J. MAIN & CO. supply every description of Garden Requisites, including—

Wire Archways and Flower Trainers,
Ornamental Iron and Wire Hurdles,
Flower Baskets and Stands in great variety,
Pea and Seed Protectors,
Garden Stakes and Pea Trainers
Floral Tools and Garden Hand Lights,
Garden Seats, Chairs, and Tables,
Lawn Mowers, Rollers, and Hose Reels,
Wrought-Iron Wine Bins,
Croquet and Lawn Tennis,
Improved Portable Steps for Libraries, etc.

Galvanized Wire Netting, etc., fixed on Railings.

A. & J. M. & Co. also supply MANGLES, WRINGING and WASHING MACHINES, by all the Best Makers.

Entrance and Field Gates, Iron and Steel Wire for Fencing Purposes, Game-Proof Wire Netting, etc. etc.

Price Lists supplied Free on application.

This business at number 31 Grassmarket sold all sorts of iron products.

Look at the three extracts below. They are from street directories for Granton, from 1881 to 1884. Look closely at the types of job people did. What do these clues tell you about where Granton was located?

Many of the people work in jobs connected with the sea. For example, Donald Macdonald was a boatman and W. Scott was a ship carpenter. These clues suggest that Granton is on the coast.

Granton 1881-2
(Cramond District)

East Cottages

M'Adie, Robert (H.M.C.)

Geddes, John, shore dues collector

Macdonald, Donald, boatman

M'Kelvie, Archibald

M'Kelvie, Mrs, refreshment rooms

M'Adie, George (H.M.C.)

Scott, W., ship carpenter

Landles, W., timber measurer

Morrison, Captain William

Granton 1882-3
(Cramond District)

East Cottages

M'Adie, Robert (H.M.C.)

Geddes, John, shore dues collector

Macdonald, Donald, boatman

M'Kelvie, Archibald

Scott, Miss C.

M'Adie, George (H.M.C.)

Scott, W., ship carpenter

Landles, W., timber measurer

Reid, A., contractor

Morrison, Captain William

Granton 1883-4
(Cramond District)

East Cottages

M'Adie, Robert (H.M.C.)

Geddes, John, shore dues collector

Macdonald, Donald, boatman

M'Kelvie, Archibald

Scott, Miss C.

M'Adie, George (H.M.C.)

Scott, W., ship carpenter

Landles, W., timber measurer

Reid, A., contractor

Morrison, Captain William

You can find out how people equipped their homes by looking at adverts like this one.

This photograph, taken in 1880, shows that Granton was a port.

Look for changes in the people who lived in the cottages between 1881 and 1884. In 1881–2 Mrs M'Kelvie had refreshment rooms in her cottage but in the next year her cottage has been taken over by Miss C. Scott. What happened to Mrs M'Kelvie? You might find out by looking in other **documents**, such as the **census** (see page 16).

Look again at the Granton street directories.

🐾 Can you find out what the letters H.M.C. stand for? What job did Robert and George M'Adie do?

🐾 Why do you think W. Landles would have had plenty of work in Granton?

When you are looking at a street directory, ask yourself questions like this:

- What type of job is listed most often?
- What businesses advertised in the directory?
- Who arrived in or left the street you are investigating in a particular year?

The census

Street directories tell us the names of the **householders**. To find out more about the other people who lived in a house, you have to look at a **census**.

A census is a questionnaire that the government sends to every householder, every ten years. The householder has to give information about everyone who lives in the house. This includes their names, ages and the jobs they do.

The first census was carried out in 1801. The most recent one was in 2001.

Road, street or name of house	Name and surname	Relation to head of family	Condition as to marriage	Age last birthday	Profession or occupation	Where born
Vicarage	Thomas A. Bushnell	Head	Married	66	Vicar of Beenham	Berkshire, Beenham
	Emily Bushnell	Wife	Married	76		
	Emily Bushnell	Daughter	Single	35		Berkshire, Beenham
	Margaret Bushnell	Daughter	Single	34		Berkshire, Beenham
	Lydia Smith	Servant	Single	30	Cook and domestic servant	Cambridgeshire, Wisbech
	Lucy Bosley	Servant	Single	40	Housemaid and domestic servant	Berkshire
	Louisa Ashby	Servant	Single	15	Domestic servant	Surrey

This is an extract from the census of 1881. It tells us who was living in the vicarage in the village of Beenham, Berkshire, in that year.

This is the vicarage at Beenham. We can find out who lived there during the 1800s by looking at the censuses.

Gravestones can provide more evidence about the families that you are investigating.

From the census extract on page 16, we can see that Thomas Bushnell was married to Emily and they had two grown-up daughters, Emily and Margaret. Neither daughter was married.

🐾 There is an important difference between the people who lived in the vicarage in 1881 and most modern families. What do you think it is?

Town and village life

You can use the census to find out what were the important industries and businesses in an area. To do this, you have to look at the jobs people did, and how many people did each type of job.

1851 Abbeydale Census
Ecclesiastical District of Ecclesall, Borough of Sheffield

Name or no. of house	Name and surname of each person who abode in the house on the Night of the 30th March 1851	Relation to head of family	Condition	Age	Rank, Profession or Occupation	Where born
1 Abbeydale Works	William Tyzack	Head	Married	35	Scythe manufacturing employing 30 men	Yorks, Ecclesall
	Fanny Tyzack	Wife	Married	36		Derbyshire, Norton
	Anne Tyzack	Daughter	Single	8		Yorks, Ecclesall
	Fanny Tyzack	Daughter	Single	6		"
	William Tyzack	Son	Single	4		"
	Frank Tyzack	Son	Single	6 mths		"
	Joshua Tyzack	Brother	Single	34		"
5 Abbeydale House	Robert Newbold	Head	Married	30	American Merchant in Cutlery	Warwicks, Coventry
	Avenilda Newbold	Wife	Married	26		Yorks, Sheffield
	Sarah Watkinson	Servant	Single	28	Servant, cook	Yorks, Sheffield
	Eliza Bolsover	Servant	Single	24	Housemaid	Derbys, Norton
	James Cope	Servant	Single	28	Groom	Shrops, Shrews
7 Abbeydale	Thomas Greaves	Head	Married	26	Scythe smith	Derbys, Norton
	Hannah Greaves	Wife	Married	24		Yorks
	Elisa Greaves	Daughter	Single	3		Derbys, Norton
	Thomas Greaves	Son	Single	3 mths		Yorks, Ecclesall

The original censuses were hand written and they are often hard to read. You have to look at them very carefully to find the clues you need.

The Abbeydale Census for 1851 shows us that William Tyzack was a **scythe** manufacturer and Thomas Greaves was a scythe smith. Robert Newbold sold cutlery to American companies. All these products were made from steel. There are the remains of a steel mill in the centre of Abbeydale. Steel was forged into products such as scythes there.

🐾 Find Norton, Ecclesall, Abbeydale and Sheffield on a map. Were most people in the 1851 census born close to Abbeydale?

🐾 Do you think the Greaves family had lived in Abbeydale for a long time?

This scene shows a blacksmith hammering red-hot metal in his forge. It was painted by Joseph Wright of Derby in 1771.

This modern photograph shows the remains of the forge at Abbeydale. The tools the worker is using suggest that metalworking had changed a great deal since Joseph Wright made his painting.

School logbooks

If you know when and where a photograph was taken, you can use the school logbook to try to find out more. This photograph shows class II at Ackworth Girls' School in 1899.

You might like to do a project on the history of your school, or find out about the children and teachers in an old school photograph. School logbooks are the place to look for lots of fascinating evidence about school life.

Headteachers used to write in their school logbooks about special events, holidays, times of illness and the punishments they have given out. The logbooks also show what kinds of lessons were taught and how many pupils went to the school.

On the opposite page you can read some extracts from school logbooks. It shows you what kind of information you might find.

15 March 1895
For the past week or more I have given out daily doses of ammoniated tincture of quinine to many children with colds and in many cases with beneficial results.

9 October 1882
It was found that 130 children were suffering from Measles. The school was closed.

2 October 1882
Typhoid fever has broken out in the area.

17 June 1887
Many fainting fits over the past few weeks. The most serious was Claire Luckin, apparently fresh and healthy at school on May 16, taken ill during the night, died on May 31 of 'inflammation of the brain'.

These extracts show how common it was in Victorian times for children to become ill or even to die. Schools often had to be closed to try to stop diseases such as measles from spreading.

Who are these boys? What was their life at school like? The school logbook provides a starting point for an investigation.

The extracts below show you some of the other reasons why children did not go to school, apart from illness.

27 February 1874	*Owing to the rain . . . many of the roads were flooded and many children were not able to attend school.*
18 December 1876	*Annie Frost still away . . . to look after younger sister who is also staying away because she has no shoes.*
2 January 1877	*It was decided at the last committee meeting to present with a half-penny each child who attends school and is present at prayers every time the school is opened during the week.*

In Victorian times many parents thought it was more important for their children to earn money or help at home than go to school.

17 April 1872
Thin attendance this week on account of hop-tying.

6 October 1873
Attendance low due to hop-picking.

25 April 1875
Many boys absent helping erect the hop poles.

24 August 1945
School closed today because of the hop-picking.

These schoolchildren who lived in Kent in 1901 earned extra money by helping to pick hops.

3 November 1873	*Visitors. His Grace the Archbishop of Canterbury visited the school today.*
3 August 1874	*Attendance low. The reason: a Grand Circus being at Tunbridge Wells and a cricket match at Penshurst.*
1946	*Funeral of Field Marshal Lord Gort VC. Children watched . . . as the military funeral is of historical interest.*

Special events

A school logbook gives you clues about special events and customs that were important in your area in the past. You could use these as the starting point for a project.

Recent logbooks are kept in the school. You will find older logbooks in the local Record Office. (Look at pages 10–11 to find out how to get them).

This is a poster for a travelling circus. Shows like these were very popular in Victorian times. Children might have had a day off school to go to the circus.

Photographs and postcards

Photographs provide history detectives with some very useful evidence, but you need to be careful how you use them.

Look at the photographs below. The top one was taken in 1996. The bottom one was taken in 1910. You might think lots of changes would have taken place in over eighty years. But the scene looks almost the same.

What clues in the photographs tell you that one was taken quite recently and one was taken a long time ago?

St Leonard's Square in Wallingford, Oxfordshire, in 1996 (left).

St Leonard's Square in 1910 (below).

When you look at a photograph you need to ask yourself two questions:

1 What does the photographer want me to see in this photograph? It might be a person, a building, or an event – anything that the photographer was deliberately trying to show. **Historians** call this the 'witting testimony' of a photograph.

2 What else in this picture is useful to me as a history detective? For example, what type of clothes are people wearing? What type of transport can you see? How do the buildings look? How do the streets look? Historians call this the 'unwitting testimony'.

What clues in the two photographs on this page help you to work out which is the modern scene and which is the scene from the past?

Wallingford Market Square in 1996.

Wallingford Market Square in 1910.

You might not think old postcards could be useful evidence for a history detective – but you would be wrong! Ask older members of your family if they have any old postcards hidden away in a drawer or a family album. You might also find them at markets, antiques fairs or car-boot sales.

Sometimes postcards have the date written on them. If not, you have to use your detective skills to work out roughly when they were produced. You might need to use a magnifying glass to see some of the smaller details.

A postcard of London.

THE PROMENADE & NORTH HILL, MINEHEAD.

206,893

Look at the postcard of Minehead above.

👣 What do you think the weather was like when the photograph was taken?

👣 What clues might you use to work out when the photograph was taken?

Look at the postcard of London on page 26. It is a view of the Houses of Parliament. Are there any clues that might tell us when the photograph was taken?

Look at the hansom cabs (bottom left), which were horse-drawn taxis. There is also an open-topped bus, pulled by horses, heading towards the photographer. You could use reference books or the Internet to find out when this kind of transport was used. In fact, the postcard shows London in the late nineteenth or early twentieth century.

Changing settlements

Your project might be about a single building or street but it would still be useful to find out why the town or village around it first grew. It might help you to understand the history of the street or building you are investigating.

When people looked for a place to settle, they needed somewhere with a water supply – near a river or spring, for example. They also needed materials to build homes – perhaps a site near a wood. Wood could be used to make fires for heating and cooking, too.

These men are Welsh coal miners. Many towns in Wales developed because coal was discovered nearby.

People also needed a place that could be defended easily, in case they were attacked. They often chose hilltops or the point where two rivers met.

Many early settlements did not survive. Perhaps all the trees were chopped down, or the water supply dried up so the people had to leave.

Other settlements survived and grew. Often, it was because there was good land for farming. In some places coal, iron ore, tin or other **minerals** were found in the ground. A mine was opened and a settlement grew up around it.

This photograph shows Glamorgan in South Wales in 1920. The scene is of a large, busy coal mine.

This photograph shows Glamorgan in 1967. The coal mine has closed. The machinery and the railway lines have been taken away.

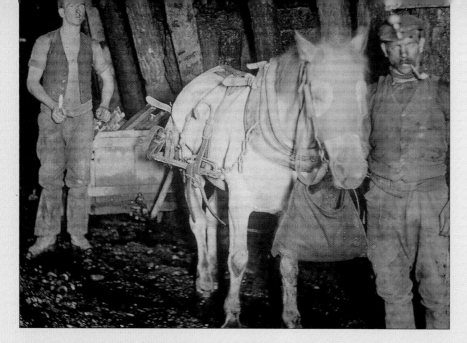

Pit ponies were used to haul the coal along the tunnels underground.

The stone above the mine entrance shows this mine opened in 1925. It had closed by 1967, when this photograph was taken.

The photographs of Welsh coal mining towns on these pages and on page 29 show how a settlement can grow and then decline.

Coal-mining settlements grew quickly in the nineteenth century. People needed coal to heat their homes and to power the steam-driven machinery in the new factories. Roads were laid so that horses and carts could carry away the coal from the mine. Later, railways were invented. Now the coal could be taken away by train.

The miners and their families needed a place to live. Cottages were built, close to the mine because the miners had to walk to work. The miners and their families also needed shops, schools and a church or chapel. The settlement grew.

If you live in a mining area, you could investigate the history of a local mine. Old photographs and maps will show you where the mine used to be. Is anything left at the site, or have new buildings been put up?

Duffryn Rhondda Colliery (above), in Wales, closed in 1972. If you look at the photograph of the working mine (below), in 1924, you can see a flight of steps. You can see them in the top photo too. The photographs show the same place.

Buildings

History detectives can find out a lot about a settlement just by going for a walk around it. Buildings provide a lot of clues.

Most of the houses in your town or village are probably built of brick or stone. Before the 1600s, most houses were built of wood. Not many of these houses have survived because the wood has rotted away.

One of the oldest buildings in your area is probably the church. There might be an old manor house, too. Important buildings like this were built of stone, so some of them have survived for hundreds of years.

Little Moreton Hall in Cheshire is more than 500 years old. It is built mainly of wood.

In the early 1800s towns grew quickly around mines and factories. In some towns you might still find the rows of small houses where the miners and factory workers lived.

When railways were built, the wealthier people could afford to live further away from the town centre and catch the train to work. You might be able to find their houses too. They were larger and more comfortable than those the ordinary workers lived in.

These houses in Bath were built in the 1700s using stone from local quarries.

These pictures give you some clues to help you work out the age of buildings in your area.

Before 1465
The houses were small. Most were built of wood, with roofs of **thatch** or split stone.

1485–1603
Houses built in Tudor times often have one floor jutting out over another. They have small doors. Windows are uneven shapes. Glass was expensive, so window panes are small.

1714–1830
In Georgian times more houses were built of stone. Georgian houses have large windows with small rectangular panes. The windows slide up or down to open. There are often fan lights over the front door.

1837–1901

Many Victorian houses were built of brick, with slate roofs. Sometimes there were patterns in the brickwork. Many schools were built around 1870 and a lot of churches were rebuilt in Victorian times.

1900–1940

Houses were built of brick and sometimes decorated with '**pebble-dash**'. Many windows opened sideways. From 1936, some houses had garages built beside them. Town councils built houses on the edge of towns. These houses all had the same design.

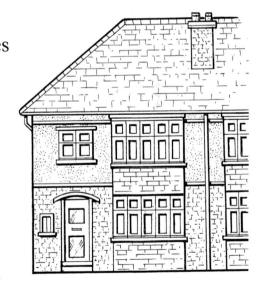

1940–today

Houses are built of brick and often have large windows. Many houses have garages. Instead of coal fires, houses have central heating, so few of them have chimneys. Steel and concrete is used to build very tall buildings.

A secret code

A quick way to record the evidence you have collected about buildings is to use a code so that you don't have to write out long descriptions. Then you can note down the codes on a map of your area.

Your secret code will show these features of a building:
- Material: what is it made from?
- Roof: what is the roof made from?
- Storeys: how many storeys (floors) does it have?
- Type: is it **detached, semi-detached** or **terraced**?
- Use: what is it used for?
- Age: how old is it?

Who lives in this building? There is a big clue in the picture.

Material
1. Brick
2. Stone
3. Wood
4. Flint
5. Brick & Stone
6. Brick & Wood
7. Other

Roof
A. Tile
B. Slate
C. Split stone
D. Thatch

Storeys
1. One storey
2. Two storeys
3. Three storeys

Type
A. Detached
B. Semi-detached
C. Terraced

Use
1. House
2. Church
3. Pub
4. Community hall
5. School
6. Shop
7. Other

Age
A. Before 1500
B. Tudor
C. Georgian
D. Victorian
E. Edwardian
F. Modern

A thatched cottage built in Tudor times.

To use the code, first have a good look at the building. Then make a note of the codes for its features in the correct order. The codes for the building in this photograph would look like this:

$$\frac{\text{5 D 2}}{\text{A 1 B}}$$

The first three codes are written on the top and the second three on the bottom. This is what it tells you about the building:

MATERIAL	ROOF	STOREYS
Brick and stone	Thatch	Two
5	D	2
A	1	B
Detached	House	Tudor
TYPE	USE	AGE

When you get home, you can plot the codes on to a sketch map like the one below. You could compare your map with old maps from different periods, to see when streets and buildings are first shown. You can find old maps in your local library.

🐾 Can you describe the buildings marked on the map below, using the codes as clues?

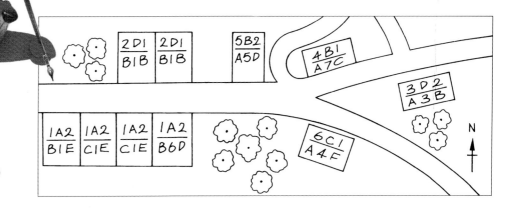

Talking about the past

Talking to people who have lived in your area for a long time is a great way of gathering evidence for your project. You could ask older relatives or family friends how your town or village has changed since they were children.

Another topic you might want to ask people about is their school days, or the jobs they used to do. Friends and relatives who are more than 70 years old might be able to remember what life was like during the Second World War.

Your great granny might have done all sorts of unusual jobs during the Second World War.

She might have been a mechanic, a pilot, or a truck driver.

How are you going to remember what people tell you? Making a tape recording, or a video recording, is a good way of collecting evidence. Another way is to make some notes as the person is talking.

Think of some questions to ask – what sort of evidence will be helpful for your project? To be a top-class history detective, you should check the information people tell you. You might need to look in school logbooks, for example, or in old newspapers. Sometimes people's memories of the past aren't quite accurate.

Great granny might have been a farm worker during the Second World War.

Can you find out why this cow was painted white during the Second World War?

The church

The church is often the oldest surviving building in a settlement. Newer churches, like United Reformed churches, Baptist churches and Methodist chapels, might have a foundation stone on the wall. This tells you when the church or chapel was built.

The writing on memorials and gravestones can tell you about families that have lived in the area for many years. You can also find out how old people were when they died – it was quite common for children to die, even in the early 1900s.

🐾 This monument is in Edinburgh. What does it tell you about how the Marquis of Argyle died? (You might need to use a magnifying glass.)

🐾 Can you find out what the letters J.P. on this **foundation stone** mean?

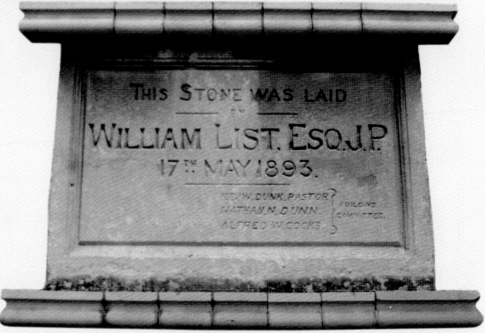

If you ask, you might be able to look at some of the church records. Often, there is a list of all the **clergymen** who have worked at the church. This can give you a clue to how old the church is.

(🐾) This is a 'sanctuary knocker' from a church door in Lancashire. Can you find out what it was used for?

Records in the church at Eyam (below) in Derbyshire show that 262 of the 350 people who lived in the village died of plague in 1665.

The first victim of the Plague died here
GEORGE VICARS
a travelling tailor lodged in this cottage with Mrs Cooper a miners widow and her two sons. He died SEPT, 7TH 1665.
EDWARD COOPER
The second victim died here SEPT, 22ND 1665.
JOHNATHAN COOPER
also a victim died here OCTOBER 28TH 1665.

(🐾) What job did the first **plague** victim in Eyam do?

Other clues

Thousands of men and women died in the two world wars in the twentieth century. In most towns and villages there is a war memorial to the people who died.

You could investigate the people whose names are written on your local war memorial. The censuses for 1891 and 1901 might give you more clues about people who died in the First World War (1914–1918). You could also look in street directories, school logbooks and old newspapers. A project like this will give you an idea of the terrible loss suffered by families all over Britain.

Your local war memorial might be in the town or village centre, near the church, or inside the church.

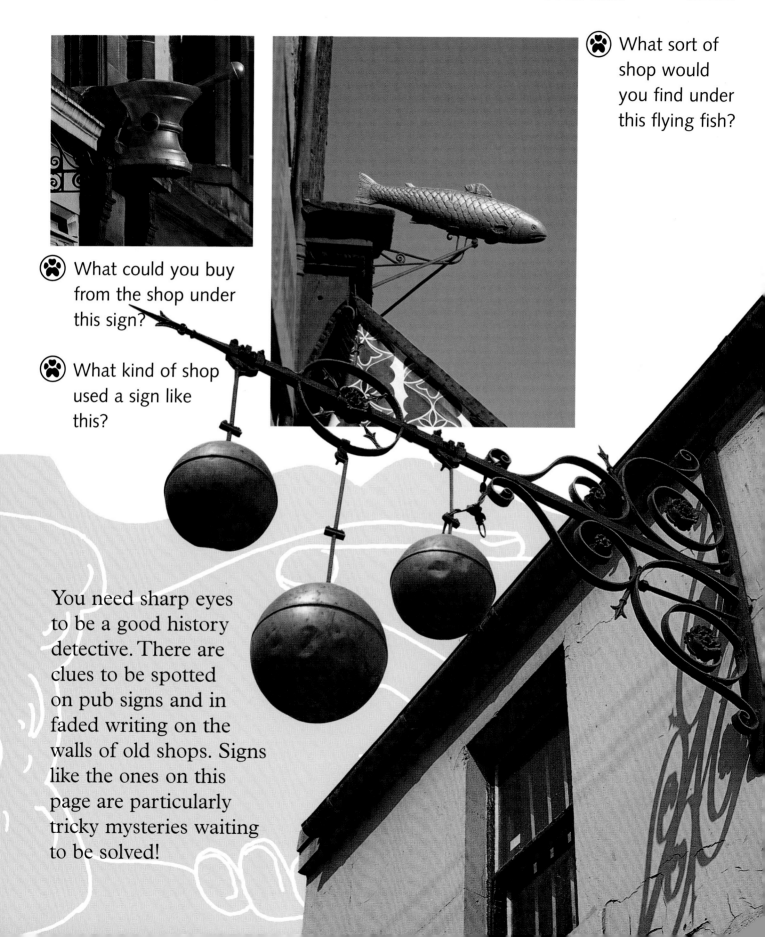

What sort of shop would you find under this flying fish?

What could you buy from the shop under this sign?

What kind of shop used a sign like this?

You need sharp eyes to be a good history detective. There are clues to be spotted on pub signs and in faded writing on the walls of old shops. Signs like the ones on this page are particularly tricky mysteries waiting to be solved!

Solving a mystery

Have you decided what local history mystery you are going to investigate? You should now know what kind of evidence you need and where to look for clues. Here are a few more useful tips:

- Choose a mystery that you can investigate without having to travel too far from home.
- Check when you can visit churches, libraries and **Record Offices**. It might be easier to visit during school holidays, as some places are closed at weekends.
- When you find a useful document or photograph, make a note of where you found it and the date when it was written or taken.

These men are loading hops into a building where they will be dried, ready to make into beer. Can you remember what these buildings are called?

PADDOCK WOOD

HOP FIELDS

Don't forget to present your evidence clearly in your project. Draw neat sketch maps. Try to include photographs or pictures and give them a caption and a date.
Most important of all – enjoy yourself!

Many of these buildings are not used any more. They have been made into houses instead – like the building shown on page 4.

Glossary

archivist The person who looks after the documents in a Record Office.

census A questionnaire sent to every householder by the government, every ten years. Historians cannot look at censuses carried out less than a hundred years ago because the people who answered it might still be alive.

clergymen The religious leaders who lead services in churches. They are also known as vicars, priests, rectors and ministers.

detached A house that is not joined on to another house.

documents Any kind of writing, such as letters, birth certificates, official reports and newspapers.

foundations The base of a building, which provides support.

foundation stone A stone set into a wall. Writing on the stone says when work on the building was begun and sometimes, who paid for it to be built.

historian A person who studies history.

hops Plants that are used to flavour beer.

householder The person who owns or rents a house.

minerals Natural substances such as iron ore, coal, tin and copper, which are found in the ground. They can be made into useful products.

parish The smallest area with a local council, often centred on a church.

pebble-dash Small stones set in plaster, which covers the outside of a house.

plague A disease that killed thousands of people.

Record Office A government office where important documents (records) are kept.

scythe A tool with a long handle and a curved blade, used for cutting grass and other crops.

semi-detached A house that is joined to another house on one side.

terraced A house that is joined to other houses on both sides, in a long row.

thatch Plants such as straw or reeds, used to cover the roof of a house.

Further information

Many official documents are available on the Internet but you must get your parents' permission before using it. You might need their help to use the sites too. Try the following:

http://www.pro.gov.uk
This is the website for the Public Record Office. It is a good starting point as it tells you what records it keeps and where to look for records it does not keep.

http://www.familyrecords.gov.uk
This site tells you how to find family information such as birth, marriage and death certificates, census information and records of emigration.

http://www.census.pro.gov.uk
You can search the 1901 census at this site, although you do have to pay for detailed information.

Another useful source of information is your local library, which will probably have a section on local history. There might be a local history group in your area, too. If you contact them, they might be able to help you with your investigation.

Answers

Page 5

The industry was brewing. Hops that are used to flavour beer were grown in the hop fields, shown on the signpost. They were taken to the oast houses and dried. Then brewers used them to make beer. The shield on the pub sign shows pictures of sheaves of barley, which is also used in beer-making, and beer barrels.

Page 7

There used to be an airfield near Reading. It was called Woodley Aerodrome and aircraft flew from there during the Second World War. The newspaper report is about the Battle of Britain, when British pilots fought to prevent the Germans from getting control of the skies over Britain. The streets are all named after types of aircraft. The pub sign shows a wartime aircraft called a Spitfire.

Page 8

The well was a gift from an Indian prince or 'maharajah'. A visitor from England had told him there was a water shortage in this area of Oxfordshire.

Page 9

Before there were town fire brigades, each insurance company had its own firefighters. They only put out fires in houses displaying the company's 'firemark' – a metal sign like the ones in the pictures. The house owner was given the firemark when he paid his insurance money to the company.

Page 11

The reference number for Crookham School is C/EL36/1-3.

Page 15

H.M.C. stands for Her (or His) Majesty's Customs. Robert and George M'Adie collected the taxes that had to be paid on certain goods that were brought into the country by ship.

W. Landles was a timber measurer – he would have had plenty of work measuring the wood used to build and repair ships.

Page 17

Three of the people who lived with the Bushnell family were servants.

Page 19

Yes. People did not move around the country so much in 1851.

The Greaves family had not lived in Abbeydale for long. We can tell this because Elisa, who was only three years old, was born in Norton, not the Ecclesall district.

Page 24

In the colour photograph you can see a car, modern road signs and road markings, a traffic island in the centre of the square and a person wearing a T-shirt and jeans.

Page 25

Clues you can use to work out which is the modern scene and which is the scene from 1910 include the type of vehicles, the clothes people are wearing, the signs on the shop fronts and the road markings.

Page 27

The shadows show it was a sunny day. The best clue is the clothes people are wearing. If you looked for the styles in a reference book you would find they are from the 1920s or 1930s.

Page 36

The building is a dovecote, where doves are kept.

Page 37

Top row, left to right: two stone houses with one storey and thatched roofs, Tudor period; brick and stone Victorian school with slate roof, two storeys; one-storey Georgian building with flint walls and slate roof.
Bottom row, left to right: two-storey brick semi-detached house with tiled roof, Edwardian period; two brick terraced houses with tiled roofs, Edwardian; two-storey Victorian shop, built of brick with tiled roof, semi-detached; modern community hall, one storey, built of

brick and wood with split stone roof; Tudor pub, two storeys, built of wood with thatched roof.

Page 39

🐾 Drivers could only use shaded headlights, or none at all, during the war, in case the lights helped enemy bombers to find their targets. Street lights were not used either. The farmer thought that painting the cow white might prevent it being run over in the dark!

Page 40

🐾 The Marquis of Argyle was beheaded.

🐾 J.P. stands for Justice of the Peace – the person who laid the stone was a local judge or 'magistrate'.

Page 41

🐾 In medieval times people who were accused of breaking the law could ask for protection in the church if they struck the knocker. This was called claiming sanctuary.

🐾 The first plague victim in Eyam was a travelling tailor (someone who made clothes).

Page 43

🐾 The sign top-left is a mortar and pestle, which chemists used to mix ingredients. So you could buy medicines here.

🐾 The flying fish sign was above a fishmonger.

🐾 Three golden balls were the sign for a pawnbroker – a place where you could hand over your valuables (such as jewellery or ornaments) in exchange for money. If you were able to pay back the money within a certain time, you could get your possessions back. If you couldn't pay back the money, the pawnbroker sold your possessions.

Index